BBC earth

DO YOU KNOW?

Level 4

PREDATORS AND PREY

Inspired by BBC Earth TV series and developed with input from BBC Earth natural history specialists

CW01064997

Written by Alex Woolf
Text adapted by Hannah Fish
Series Editor: Nick Coates

LADYBIRD BOOKS

UK | USA | Canada | Ireland | Australia
India | New Zealand | South Africa

Ladybird Books is part of the Penguin Random House group of companies
whose addresses can be found at global.penguinrandomhouse.com.
www.penguin.co.uk   www.puffin.co.uk   www.ladybird.co.uk

Penguin
Random House
UK

First published 2020
001

Text copyright © Ladybird Books Ltd, 2020

All images copyright © BBC 2015 excluding:
image on page 4 (bottom) copyright © e2dan/Shutterstock.com
image on page 4 (cacti) copyright © Franciele Rodrigues /Shutterstock.com
image on page 4 (camouflage) copyright © vicspacewalker/Shutterstock.com
image on page 4 (fin) copyright © Photograph by Jonathan Smith © BBC NHU 2017
image on page 4 (grasslands) copyright ©Photograph by Chadden Hunter © BBC NHU 2016
image on page 5 (poison) copyright © pelfophoto/Shutterstock.com
image on page 5 (smell) copyright © bimka/Shutterstock.com
image on page 5 (speed) copyright © JonathanC Photography/Shutterstock.com
image on page 5 (trap) copyright © josehidalgo87/Shutterstock.com
image on page 6–7 (elephant background) copyright © Photograph by Bruce Ellis/Shutterstock.com
Image on page 4 (hunt), image on page 5 (predator), image on page 5 (prey), image on page 7 (grasslands),
image on page 8–9 (golden eagle), image on page 13 (harris hawk and harris hawk hunting),
image on page 23 (Nubian ibex on cliff), image on page 28–29 (field background) copyright © BBC 2016
image on page 7 and 30 (lion), image on page 7 (zebra), image on page 10 (meerkats),
image on page 10–11 (African hunting dogs, background), image on page 11 (African hunting dogs),
image on page 12 (striated caracara), image on page 17 (tiger shark), image on page 17 (archer fish),
image on page 19 (mimic octopus) copyright © BBC 2014
image on page 11 (ververt monkey) copyright © Amelandfoto/Shutterstock.com
image on page 13 (squirrel) copyright © Charles T. Peden/Shutterstock.com
image on pages 12–13 and 30 (orca), image on page 26 (cuttlefish changing colours), image on page 27 (cuttlefish),
image on page 27 (cuttlefish mesmerising crab) copyright © BBC 2017
image on pages 14–15 (poison dart frog) copyright © Dirk Ercken/Shutterstock.com
image on page 15 (bombardier beetle) copyright © Samrarn Chaipichitpun/Shutterstock.com
image on page 15 (spitting cobra) copyright © Eugene Troskie/Shutterstock.com
image on page 15 (skunk) copyright © Geoffrey Kuchera/Shutterstock.com
image on pages 19 and 31 (zebra) copyright © RemcoZ/Shutterstock.com
image on pages 18–19 (arctic hare, background) copyright © Chanonry/Shutterstock.com
image on page 21 (peregrine falcon, in flight), image on page 21 (peregrine falcon, caught prey) copyright © Collins93/Shutterstock.com
image on page 21 (shortfin mako shark) copyright © wildestanimal/Shutterstock.com
image on page 26–27 (cuttlefish background) copyright © Justin Hoffman © BBC 2017
image on page 27 and 31 (striated heron) Patrice Correia / Biosphoto, BIOSPHOTO / Alamy Stock Photo
image on page 28 (opossum) copyright © Agnieszka Bacal/Shutterstock.com
image on page 29 (potoo bird) copyright © Uwe Bergwitz/Shutterstock.com
image on page 29 (kallima butterfly) copyright © Fabien Monteil/Shutterstock.com

BBC and BBC Earth (word marks and logos) are trademarks of the British Broadcasting Corporation and are used under licence.
BBC logo © 1996, BBC Earth logo © 2014

Printed in China

A CIP catalogue record for this book is available from the British Library

ISBN: 978–0–241–38290–5

All correspondence to:
Ladybird Books Ltd
Penguin Random House Children's
One Embassy Gardens, New Union Square
5 Nine Elms Lane, London SW8 5DA

Contents

New words

bottom
(noun)

cactus
(cacti)

camouflage
(noun)

fin

grasslands

hunt
(verb)

poison
(noun)

predator

prey
(noun)

smell
(verb)

speed

trap
(noun)

What is a food chain?

Every day, animals need to find enough food to eat, and they need to stay safe from other animals.

In every place where animals live, there is a food chain. A food chain is what eats what.

This is a food chain in the **grasslands**.

At the top of the food chain are big **predators**, like lions. Nothing eats them.

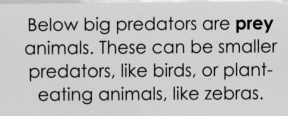

Below big predators are **prey** animals. These can be smaller predators, like birds, or plant-eating animals, like zebras.

At the bottom of the food chain are the plants that animals eat, like grass.

 PROJECT

Work in a group.
Talk with a friend about sharks, seagrass and sea turtles. What eats what, do you think? Draw a food chain like the one above to show your answers.

How does a predator use its senses?

A predator uses its eyes, ears, nose, mouth and body to find prey. It uses its senses.

Different animals use different senses because they live in different places and **hunt** in different ways.

Eagles must find their prey from high in the sky, so they have very good eyes.

Some wolves hunt at night. They use their noses to find food.

web

A spider can feel when an insect flies into its web.

 **FIND OUT!**

Use books or the internet to find one animal that uses its sense of hearing to hunt for food.

How do animals stay safe?

Many prey animals work together to stay safe.

Meerkats live in groups. Some meerkats watch for predators.

When a meerkat sees a predator, it calls to the other meerkats, and they all run back to their homes.

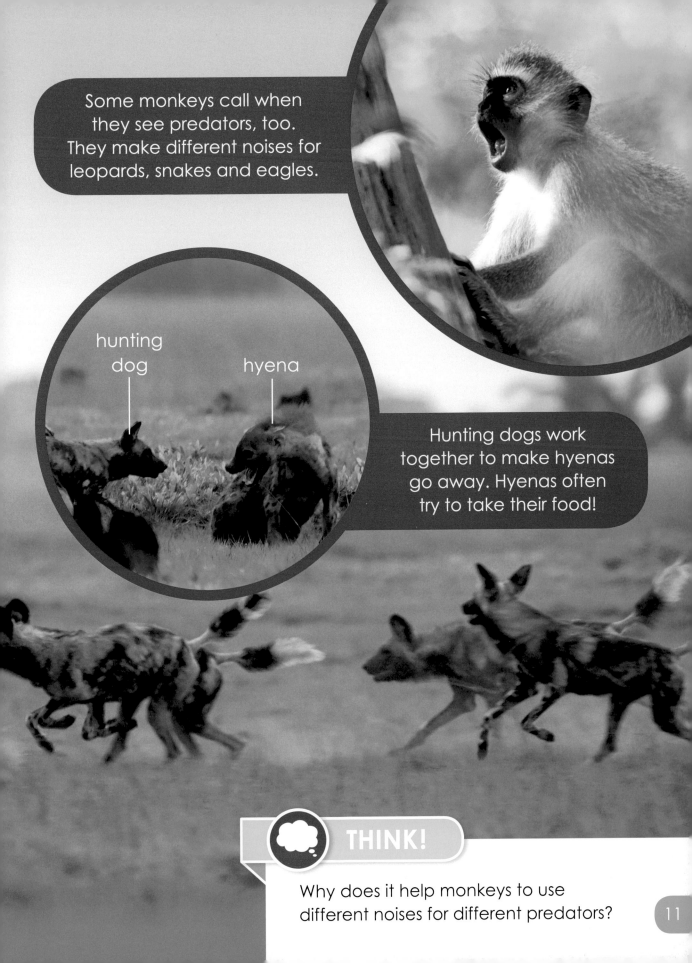

Some monkeys call when they see predators, too. They make different noises for leopards, snakes and eagles.

hunting dog

hyena

Hunting dogs work together to make hyenas go away. Hyenas often try to take their food!

THINK!

Why does it help monkeys to use different noises for different predators?

How do predators work together?

Many predators also work together to hunt their prey.

Orcas swim in circles around big groups of herrings. They push the herrings into smaller groups. Then, it is easier to catch the herrings.

Some birds, like these caracaras, work in groups to take seabird eggs.

Harris hawks hunt in groups to catch ground squirrels. The squirrels hide in **cacti**.

First, the hawks fly around to make the squirrels leave the cacti.

If this does not work, the hawks go into the cacti. The squirrels cannot run away because the hawks are all around them.

▶ WATCH!

Watch the video (see page 32).
How many orcas are there?
How do orcas use their tails when they are hunting herrings?

Which frog is **bad** to eat?

Some prey animals stay safe by using **poison** or venom to hurt predators.

The poison dart frog has poison on its body. The frog's bright colours tell predators not to eat it!

Some animals use poison or venom before a predator tries to eat them.

venom

fang

Spitting cobras spray venom from their fangs into the eyes of predators.

Skunks spray from their **bottoms**. It **smells** very bad!

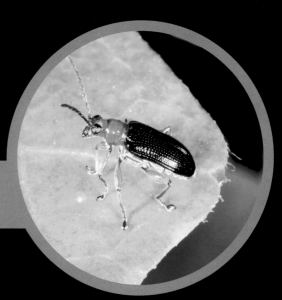

Some insects spray their predators, too.

 LOOK!

Look at the pages.
Why is the poison dart frog brightly coloured?

Which predators surprise their prey?

Many predators surprise their prey.
Polar bears do this when they hunt seals.

A seal is on the ice, and a polar bear is
suddenly jumping out of the sea to catch it.

Tiger sharks move fast to catch albatross chicks that are flying near to the sea.

The archer fish sprays water from its mouth to make insects fall into the water.

THINK!

Is it easy or difficult for predators to surprise their prey? Why?

How do animals hide from predators?

Some animals have colours that are the same as the things around them. Then predators cannot see them. This is called **camouflage**.

Arctic hares are white, so it is hard to see them in the snow.

When zebras stand together in groups, their black and white colours make it hard to see each zebra. It is difficult for predators to choose one animal to hunt.

This octopus can change the colour of its body to look the same as the rock or sea floor below it.

 **FIND OUT!**

Use books or the internet to find another example of an animal that uses camouflage so predators cannot see it.

Which predators use speed?

In the grasslands, it is hard for predators to hide. Some predators use their **speed** to catch their prey.

Cheetahs are the fastest land animals on Earth.

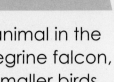

The fastest animal in the sky is the peregrine falcon, which eats smaller birds.

When it sees its prey, the peregrine falcon flies up high into the sky. Then, it comes down very quickly and catches its prey with its feet.

The shortfin mako is the fastest shark in the sea. It uses its speed to catch other fast fish, like tuna and swordfish.

PROJECT

Work in a group.

Make a one-page report on the cheetah. Include pictures and information about where it lives, its prey and the speed it can run.

Can fish fly?

Some animals do interesting things to stay safe.

When tuna hunt flying fish, the flying fish jump out of the sea. They cannot fly like birds, but their long **fins** are like wings.

Flying fish can use their fins to move above the water.

Seabirds catch and eat flying fish that jump out of the water.

This ibex stays safe in very high mountains, but there is no grass to eat there.

When it comes down from the mountains to eat, there are predators like foxes. If a predator comes near, the ibex runs fast back to the mountains.

LOOK!

Look at the pages.
Why does the ibex come down from the mountains?

Which spider builds bridges?

Some predators hunt without moving. They make **traps** for their prey. Spiders do this by building webs.

The Darwin's bark spider builds one of the largest webs. It can build its web like a bridge across a river.

First, it sprays long pieces of silk into the sky.

This silk is carried by the wind across a river to make a bridge.

silk

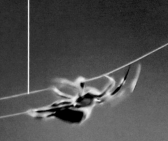

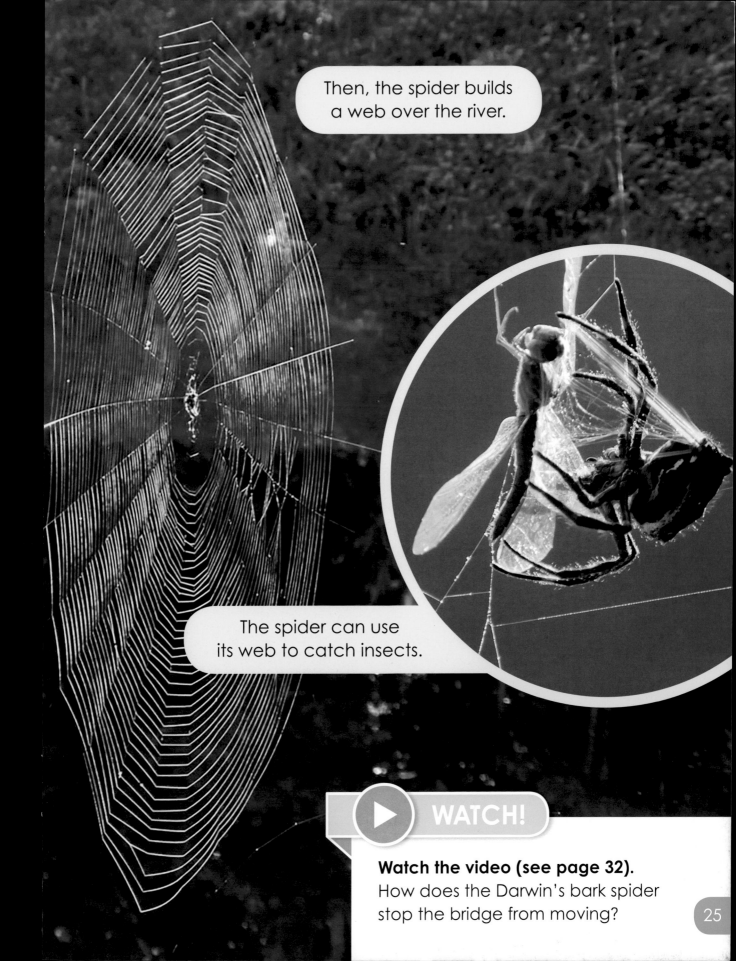

Then, the spider builds a web over the river.

The spider can use its web to catch insects.

▶ WATCH!

Watch the video (see page 32).
How does the Darwin's bark spider stop the bridge from moving?

How does a cuttlefish catch a crab?

Some predators do clever things to catch their prey.

This cuttlefish can change the colours on its body.

The crab sees the colours. The crab is so interested that it stops moving.

Then, the cuttlefish can eat the crab.

Striated herons sometimes drop insects into a river. They wait for fish to come and eat the insects, then the herons catch the fish.

▶ **WATCH!**

Watch the video (see page 32).
Why does the cuttlefish stop changing colours?

Which animal plays dead?

Prey animals also do clever things to stay safe.

When the opossum sees a predator, it falls to the ground.

The predator thinks the opossum is dead and goes away. But the opossum is just playing dead!

Some prey animals stay safe because they look the same as something else.

This bird looks like part of the tree it is sitting on.

This butterfly looks like a dead leaf.

stick insect

This stick insect looks like part of a tree.

FIND OUT!

Use books or the internet to find out which animals spray ink to distract predators.

Quiz

Choose the correct answers.

1 A food chain is . . .
   a what eats when.
   b what eats where.
   c what eats what.

2 Which of these sentences is NOT true?
   a No predators use their eyes to hunt prey.
   b Predators use their senses to hunt prey.
   c Predators hunt prey in different ways.

3 Predators work together . . .
   a to live in groups.
   b to hunt their prey.
   c to hide in cacti.

4 Polar bears and tiger sharks catch their prey using . . .
   a surprise.
   b poison.
   c fish.

5 Some animals use camouflage . . .
  a to spray venom.
  b to stop predators seeing them.
  c to smell bad.

6 Flying fish . . .
  a fly like birds.
  b jump out of the water.
  c catch seabirds.

7 Spiders build . . .
  a trees.
  b rivers.
  c webs.

8 Striated herons eat . . .
  a insects.
  b fish.
  c crabs.

Visit www.ladybirdeducation.co.uk for FREE **DO YOU KNOW?** teaching resources.

- video clips with simplified voiceover and subtitles
- video and comprehension activities
- class projects and lesson plans
- audio recording of every book
- digital version of every book
- full answer keys

To access video clips, audio tracks and digital books:

1 Go to **www.ladybirdeducation.co.uk**
2 Click "Unlock book"
3 Enter the code below

j4i79mlgPE

Stay safe online! Some of the DO YOU KNOW? activities ask children to do extra research online. Remember:

- ensure an adult is supervising;
- use established search engines such as Google or Kiddle;
- children should never share personal details, such as name, home or school address, telephone number or photos.